CHALLENGE

LECTOR HOUSE PUBLIC DOMAIN WORKS

This book is a result of an effort made by Lector House towards making a contribution to the preservation and repair of original classic literature. The original text is in the public domain in the United States of America, and possibly other countries depending upon their specific copyright laws.

In an attempt to preserve, improve and recreate the original content, certain conventional norms with regard to typographical mistakes, hyphenations, punctuations and/or other related subject matters, have been corrected upon our consideration. However, few such imperfections might not have been rectified as they were inherited and preserved from the original content to maintain the authenticity and construct, relevant to the work. The work might contain a few prior copyright references as well as page references which have been retained, wherever considered relevant to the part of the construct. We believe that this work holds historical, cultural and/or intellectual importance in the literary works community, therefore despite the oddities, we accounted the work for print as a part of our continuing effort towards preservation of literary work and our contribution towards the development of the society as a whole, driven by our beliefs.

We are grateful to our readers for putting their faith in us and accepting our imperfections with regard to preservation of the historical content. We shall strive hard to meet up to the expectations to improve further to provide an enriching reading experience.

Though, we conduct extensive research in ascertaining the status of copyright before redeveloping a version of the content, in rare cases, a classic work might be incorrectly marked as not-in-copyright. In such cases, if you are the copyright holder, then kindly contact us or write to us, and we shall get back to you with an immediate course of action.

HAPPY READING!

CHALLENGE

LOUIS UNTERMEYER

ISBN: 978-93-5420-864-5

Published: 1914

LECTOR HOUSE LLP
E-MAIL: lectorpublishing@gmail.com

CHALLENGE

BY

LOUIS UNTERMEYER

1914

Published, April, 1914

CONTENTS

III
SONGS OF PROTEST

For the privilege of reprinting many of the poems included in this volume, the author thanks the editors of *The Century, Harper's, The Forum, The Masses, The Smart Set, The Independent, The American, The Delineator, The New Age, The Poetry Journal* and other magazines.

I
SUMMONS

To
Walter Lippmann

SUMMONS

The eager night and the impetuous winds,
The hints and whispers of a thousand lures,
And all the swift persuasion of the Spring
Surged from the stars and stones, and swept me on...
The smell of honeysuckles, keen and clear,
Startled and shook me, with the sudden thrill
Of some well-known but half-forgotten voice.
A slender stream became a naked sprite,
Flashed around curious bends, and winked at me
Beyond the turns, alert and mischievous.
A saffron moon, dangling among the trees,
Seemed like a toy balloon caught in the boughs,
Flung there in sport by some too-mirthful breeze...
And as it hung there, vivid and unreal,
The whole world's lethargy was brushed away;
The night kept tugging at my torpid mood
And tore it into shreds. A warm air blew
My wintry slothfulness beyond the stars;
And over all indifference there streamed
A myriad urges in one rushing wave...
Touched with the lavish miracles of earth,
I felt the brave persistence of the grass;
The far desire of rivulets; the keen,
Unconquerable fervor of the thrush;
The endless labors of the patient worm;
The lichen's strength; the prowess of the ant;
The constancy of flowers; the blind belief
Of ivy climbing slowly toward the sun;
The eternal struggles and eternal deaths—
And yet the groping faith of every root!
Out of old graves arose the cry of life;
Out of the dying came the deathless call.
And, thrilling with a new sweet restlessness,
The thing that was my boyhood woke in me—
Dear, foolish fragments made me strong again;
Valiant adventures, dreams of those to come,
And all the vague, heroic hopes of youth,

With fresh abandon, like a fearless laugh,
Leaped up to face the heaven's unconcern...

And then—veil upon veil was torn aside—
Stars, like a host of merry girls and boys,
Danced gaily 'round me, plucking at my hand;
The night, scorning its ancient mystery,
Leaned down and pressed new courage in my heart;
The hermit thrush, throbbing with more than Song,
Sang with a happy challenge to the skies;
Love, and the faces of a world of children,
Swept like a conquering army through my blood—
And Beauty, rising out of all its forms,
Beauty, the passion of the universe,
Flamed with its joy, a thing too great for tears.
And, like a wine, poured itself out for me
To drink of, to be warmed with, and to go
Refreshed and strengthened to the ceaseless fight;
To meet with confidence the cynic years;
Battling in wars that never can be won,
Seeking the lost cause and the brave defeat!

PRAYER

God, though this life is but a wraith,
Although we know not what we use,
Although we grope with little faith,
Give me the heart to fight—and lose.

Ever insurgent let me be,
Make me more daring than devout;
From sleek contentment keep me free.
And fill me with a buoyant doubt.

Open my eyes to visions girt
With beauty, and with wonder lit—
But let me always see the dirt,
And all that spawn and die in it.

Open my ears to music; let
Me thrill with Spring's first flutes and drums—
But never let me dare forget
The bitter ballads of the slums.

From compromise and things half-done,
Keep me, with stern and stubborn pride;
And when, at last, the fight is won
God, keep me still unsatisfied.

TO ARMS!

Who can be dull or wrapped in unconcern
Knowing a world so clamorous and keen;
A world of ardent conflict, honest spleen,
And healthy, hot desires too swift to turn;
Vivid and vulgar—with no heart to learn...
See how that drudge, a thing unkempt, unclean,
Laughs with the royal laughter of a queen.
Even in her the eager fires burn.

Who can be listless in these stirring hours
When, with athletic courage, we engage
To storm, with fierce abandon, sterner powers
And meet indifference with a joyful rage;
Thrilled with a purpose and the dream that towers
Out of this arrogant and blundering age.

ON THE BIRTH OF A CHILD

(Jerome Epstein—August 8, 1912)

Lo—to the battle-ground of Life,
Child, you have come, like a conquering shout,
Out of a struggle—into strife;
Out of a darkness—into doubt.

Girt with the fragile armor of Youth,
Child, you must ride into endless wars,
With the sword of protest, the buckler of truth,
And a banner of love to sweep the stars.

About you the world's despair will surge;
Into defeat you must plunge and grope—
Be to the faltering an urge;
Be to the hopeless years a hope!

Be to the darkened world a flame;
Be to its unconcern a blow—
For out of its pain and tumult you came,
And into its tumult and pain you go.

HOW MUCH OF GODHOOD

How much of Godhood did it take—
What purging epochs had to pass,
Ere I was fit for leaf and lake
And worthy of the patient grass?

What mighty travails must have been,
What ages must have moulded me,
Ere I was raised and made akin

To dawn, the daisy and the sea.

In what great struggles was I felled,
In what old lives I labored long,
Ere I was given a world that held
A meadow, butterflies and Song?

But oh, what cleansings and what fears,
What countless raisings from the dead,
Ere I could see Her, touched with tears,
Pillow the little weary head.

THE GREAT CAROUSAL

Oh, do not think me dead when I
Beneath a bit of earth shall lie;
Think not that aught can ever kill
My arrogant and stubborn will.
My buoyant strength, my eager soul,
My stern desire shall keep me whole
And lift me from the drowsy deep...
I shall not even yield to Sleep,
For Death can never take from me
My warm, insatiate energy;
He shall not dare to touch one part
Of the gay challenge of my heart.
And I shall laugh at him, and lie
Happy beneath a laughing sky;
For I have fought too joyously
To let the conqueror conquer me—
I know that, after strengthening strife,
Death cannot quench my love of life;
Rob me of my dear self, my ears
Of music or my eyes of tears ...
No, Death shall come in friendlier guise;
The cloths of darkness from my eyes
He shall roll back, and lo, the sea
Of Silence shall not cover me.
He shall make soft my final bed,
Stand, like a servant, at my head;
And, thrilled with all that Death may give,
I shall lie down to rest—and live...

And I shall know within the earth
A softer but a deeper mirth.
The wind shall never troll a song
But I shall hear it borne along,
And echoed long before he passes
By all the little unborn grasses.

I shall be clasped by roots and rains,
Feeding and fed by living grains;
There shall not be a single flower
Above my head but bears my power,
And every butterfly or bee
That tastes the flower shall drink of me.
Ah, we shall share a lip to lip
Carousal and companionship!

The storm, like some great blustering lout,
Shall play his games with me and shout
His joy to all the country-side.
Autumn, sun-tanned and April-eyed,
Shall scamper by and send his hosts
Of leaves, like brown and merry ghosts,
To frolic over me; and stones
Shall feel the dancing in their bones.
And red-cheeked Winter too shall be
A jovial bed-fellow for me,
Setting the startled hours ringing
With boisterous tales and lusty singing.
And, like a mother that has smiled
For years on every tired child,
Summer shall hold me in her lap...
And when the root stirs and the sap
Climbs anxiously beyond the boughs,
And all the friendly worms carouse,
Then, oh, how proudly, we shall sing
Bravuras for the feet of Spring!

And I shall lie forever there
Like some great king, and watch the fair
Young Spring dance on for me, and know
That love and rosy valleys glow
Where'er her blithe feet touch the earth.
And headlong joy and reckless mirth
Seeing her footsteps shall pursue.
Oh, I shall watch her smile and strew
Laughter and life with either hand;
And every quiver of the land,
Shall pierce me, while a joyful wave
Beats in upon my radiant grave.
Aye, like a king in deathless state
I shall be throned, and contemplate
The dying of the years, the vast
Vague panorama of the past,
The march of centuries, the surge

Of ages .... but the deathless urge
Shall stir me always, and my will
Shall laugh to keep me living still;
Thrilling with every call and cry —
Too much in love with life to die.
Content to touch the earth, to hear
The whisper of each waiting year,
To help the stars go proudly by,
To speed the timid grass; and lie,
Sharing, with every movement's breath,
The rich eternity of Death.

THANKS

Thank God for this bright frailty of Life,
The lyric briefness of its reckless Spring;
Thank God for all the swift adventuring,
The bold uncertainty, the rousing strife.

Thank God the world is set to such a tune,
That life is such a proud and crashing wave;
That none, but lifeless things, shall be Time's slave,
Like the long-dead but never tiring moon;

That godlike passion strangely leaps and runs;
That youth cannot grow old, nor beauty stale;
That even Death is fragile and must fail
Before the wind of joy that speeds the suns.

GOD'S YOUTH

I often wish that I had been alive
Ere God grew old, before His eyes were tired
Of the eternal circlings of the sun;
Of the perpetual Springs; the weary years
Forever marching on an unknown quest;
The yawning seasons pacing to and fro,
Like stolid sentinels to guard the earth.
I wish that I had been alive when He
Was still delighted with each casual thing
His mind could fashion, when His soul first thrilled
With childlike pleasure at the blooming sun;
When the first dawn met His enraptured eyes,
And the first prayers of men stirred in His heart.
With what a glow of pride He heard the stars
Rush by Him singing as they bravely leaped
Into the unexplored and endless skies,
Bearing His beauty, like a battle-cry.

Or watched the light, obedient to His will,
Spring out of nothingness to answer Him,
Hurling strange suns and planets in its joy
Of fiery freedom from the lifeless dark.
But more than all the splendid heavens He made,
The elements new-tamed, the harnessed worlds;
In spite of these, it must have pleased Him most
To feel Himself branch out, let go, dare all,
Give utterance to His vaguely-formed desires,
And loose a flood of fancies, wild and frank.

Oh those were noble times; those gay attempts,
Those vast and droll experiments that were made
When God was young and blithe and whimsical.
When, from the infinite humor of His heart,
He made the elk with such extravagant horns,
The grotesque monkey-folk, the angel-fish,
That make the ocean's depths a visual heaven;
The animals like plants, the plants like beasts;
The loud, inane hyena, and the great
Impossible giraffe, whose silly head
Threatens the stars, his feet embracing earth.
The paradox of the peacock, whose bright form
Is like a brilliant trumpet, and his voice
A strident squawk, a cackle and a joke.
The ostrich, like a snake tied to a bird,
All out of sense and drawing, wilder far
Than all the mad, fantastic thoughts of men.
The hump-backed camel, like a lump of clay,
Thumbed at for hours, and then thrown aside.
The elephant, with splendid, useless tooth,
And nose and arm and fingers all in one.
The hippopotamus, absurd and bland—
Oh, how God must have laughed when first He saw
These great jests breathe and love and walk about;
And how the heavens must have echoed him...
For greater than His beauty or His wrath
Was God's vast mirth before His back was bent
With Time and all the troubling universe,
Ere He grew dull and weary with creating...
Oh, to have been alive and heard that laugh
Thrilling the stars, convulsing all the earth,
While meteors flashed from out His sparkling eyes,
And even the eternal, placid Night
Forgot to lift reproving fingers, smiled
And joined, indulgent, in the merriment...
And, how they sang, and how the hours flew

When God was young and blithe and whimsical.

IN THE BERKSHIRE HILLS

How can the village dead remain so still...
Surely they tingle with the winey air,
When the skies riot and the sunsets flare
And all the world becomes a flaming hill.
Surely the driest dust must turn and thrill
When these wild breezes sweep out all despair—
And lakes are bluest, pools are starriest where
The streaming heavens overflow and spill.

Oh, were it I that lay like any clod,
Though buried under rock and gnarled tree,
I would arise, and, through the clinging sod,
Go struggling upward, passionate and proud;
Laugh, with the winds and mountains watching me,
And dance in triumph on my crumbling shroud.

VOICES

All day with anxious heart and wondering ear
I listened to the city; heard the ground
Echo with human thunder, and the sound
Go reeling down the streets and disappear.
The headlong hours, in their wild career,
Shouted and sang until the world was drowned
With babel-voices, each one more profound...
All day it surged—but nothing could I hear.

That night the country never seemed so still;
The trees and grasses spoke without a word
To stars that brushed them with their silver wings.
Together with the moon I climbed the hill,
And, in the very heart of Silence, heard
The speech and music of immortal things.

REVELATION

September—and an afternoon
Heavy with languid thoughts and long;
The air breathes faintly, half in swoon,
Like silence trembling after Song.
The mighty calmness seems to draw
My spirit through a painless birth—
And now, with eyes that never saw,
I see the poetry of earth.

That group of old maple-trees brooding in peace by the river,

Happy with sunlight, and an oriole singing among them—
Lo, what a marvel (what rapture for Him who first sung them)
That here, in less space than a carpenter's workshop, the Giver
Has fashioned a casual wonder
Greater than dawn or the thunder.
Here in a dozen of feet He has blended
Music and motion and color and form,
Each in itself a creation so splendid
That, were it the world's one beauty, 'twould warm
And kindle all Life till it ended.

Birds and old maple-trees—
Only to think of these,
Only to dream of them here for an hour
Is to know all the secrets of earth.
For here is the world that God sang into flower
And bloom at its birth—
Here is its magical uplift and power;
Its music and mirth.

Here the sun scarcely wakes;
Like a monarch it takes
Rest on the lordliest branches alone.
Till a glad tremor shakes
Every leaf that is blown—
While a zephyr advancing,
Breathes gently and breaks
The light into dancing
Figures, with glancing
Rhythms and rhymes of their own.

Yes, here in this spot, in this edge of an acre
All of the world is, the heart and the whole of it—
Here is a universe; daily the Maker
Shows here the sweet and extravagant soul of it.
For the arms of the maple have held in their cover
The earth and the sky and the stars, every one—
Not the tenderest twig but has known, like a lover
The silence, the night and the sun.

Not the airiest bird but has sung, all unknowing,
The joy of each minstrel that carols unheard.
And Summer, green fields and a world of things growing,
Are brought to this spot by the breath of a bird.
And there's never a wind but brings road-sides and ranches,
Forests and tales of the far-off and free—
And the rush of the breeze as it sings in the branches
Echoes and answers the rush of the sea...

A group of old maple-trees brooding in peace by the river—
That—and a bird, nothing else... But above and around it,
The spell of the infinite beauty, half-hidden forever,
Lies, like a secret of God's—and here I have found it.
The hymn of the cosmic—the anthem that has for its choir
Stars, rivers and flowers—still rises and sweeps me along;
While the cry of the oriole melts in a sunset of fire
And the heavens, a jubilant chorus, are flushed with the fires of Song!

AFFIRMATION

As long as vigorous discontent
Goads us from torpid ease, or worse,
I thank the power that sent
Struggle, the savior of the universe.

As long as things are torn and hurled
In this implacable unrest,
I shall embrace the world
With joyful fierceness and undying zest.

I shall grow strong with every hurt;
The scorn, the anger will achieve
Only a glad, alert
Desire to question boldly—and believe.

My eager faith shall keep me set
Against despair or careless hate,
Knowing this smoke and sweat
Is forging something violent—and great!

DOWN-HILL ON A BICYCLE

The rolling earth stops
As I climb to the summit,
Then like a plummet
It suddenly drops...

Down, down I go—
Past rippling acres;
Hillsides like breakers
Over me flow.

Wildly alive
I hail the green shimmer,
Fresh as a swimmer
After the dive.

Like banners unfurled
The skies dip and flourish—
The keen breezes nourish,

While the bright world.

Is a ribbon unrolled
With a border of grasses;
And tansies are masses
And splotches of gold.

Still I whirl on—
Startled, a sparrow
Darts from the yarrow,
Flash—and is gone...

Faster the gleams
Die as they dazzle—
And roadsides of basil
Turn to pink streams.

Sharp as a knife
Is each perfume and color.
To feel nothing duller—
God, that were Life!

MIDNIGHT—BY THE OPEN WINDOW

How rapt the sleeping stillness of the night—
Incomparably close and vast... One might
Hear the tense silence in the little street
Reaching to heaven, where it swells and breaks
Into moon-music and star-song that makes
My senses bend and sway, as waving wheat
Trembles before the wind's majestic feet;
Trembles with happy fear and numb delight.

How sharp the silence... like a sword to smite
Brittle security and iron aches;
A soundless and imperative blast that wakes
Undreamed of powers, terrible and sweet...
While God comes down, roused to the jubilant fight;
Roused from the sleepy comfort of His seat.

THE WINE OF NIGHT

Come, drink the mystic wine of Night,
Brimming with silence and the stars,
While earth, bathed in this holy light,
Is seen without its scars.
Drink in the daring and the dews,
The calm winds and the restless gleam—
This is the draught that Beauty brews;
Drink—it is the Dream.

Drink, oh my soul, and do not yield—
These solitudes, this wild-rose air,
Shall strengthen thee, shall be thy shield,
Against a world's despair.
Oh, quaff this stirrup-cup of stars,
Trembling with hope and high desire—
Then back into the hopeless wars
With faith and fire!

II
INTERLUDES

To
My Wife

INVOCATION

Listen, my lute, I would turn from your militant measures.
Well have you answered the touch of intransigent fingers;
Wildly your strings have vibrated—but have you forgotten
How to make love-songs?

Lute, you are hot to the hand; you are tense and exultant.
Cease crying out—let me rest from the din and the battle.
Life is not only a summoning shout and a struggle,
A blow and a silence.

Is there not vigorous peace after vigorous onslaught?
Beauty's a challenge as fierce and as stirring as conflict...
Look—how she runs through the tremulous twilight to meet me—
Do you remember?

See—it is night and she turns to my arms of a sudden;
Soft as a mother and wild with the fires of April—
Bashful and bold, with her passionate hair all about her;
Lovely and lavish.

Lute, it was she who awoke and impelled us to singing—
Ah, those first lyrics, impulsive and feeble and earnest—
She who aroused us and soothed us—our passion, our pillow—
Dare you forget her!

Only remember 'tis she keeps me rested and restless;
Only remember my heart, like a fate in strong breezes.
Leaps at the thought of her voice and her slow, searching kisses,
Stabbing and healing.

"FEUERZAUBER"

I never knew the earth had so much gold—
The fields run over with it, and this hill
Hoary and old,
Is young with buoyant blooms that flame and thrill.

Such golden fires, such yellows—lo, how good
This spendthrift world, and what a lavish God—
This fringe of wood,
Blazing with buttercup and goldenrod.

You too, beloved, are changed. Again I see
Your face grow mystical, as on that night
You turned to me,
And all the trembling world—and you—were white.

Aye, you are touched; your singing lips grow dumb;
The fields absorb you, color you entire...
And you become
A goddess standing in a world of fire!

SUNDAY NIGHT

Tossing, throughout this tense and nervous night
Sleepless I drowse. My soul, for lack of rest,
Sinks like a bird, that after flight on flight
Misses the shelter of its well-loved nest.
So would I gain your side and seek, my love,
The comfortable heaven of your breast.

Once more to lie beside the window seat,
And see, far off, the ribboned river-lights,
The yellow gas-lamps in the dusky street—
And pressing close, from proud and alien heights,
The noble skies and the inviolate stars
Surround and bless us these autumnal nights.

No words—the silence and your breathless name
Are all that's in the world; and faint and fair
The distant church-bells solemnly proclaim
To all the meek and sabbath-scented air...
I take you in my arms ... and I awake
Groping, with restless anger, for a prayer.

AT KENNEBUNKPORT

We sat together at the ocean's edge,
The night was mystical and warm.
From every rambling roadside hedge
Wild roses followed us with a swarm
Of scents; the pines and every odorous tree
Triumphed and rose above the languid sea.
The stars were dim—
The world was hushed, as though before a shrine...
We sat together at the ocean's rim,
Your hand in mine.

Then came the moon—
A calm, benignant moon,
Like some indulgent mother that has smiled
On every wayward child.

The breathing stillness, like a wordless croon,
Made the soft heart of heaven doubly mild;
And the salt air mingled with the air of June...

The vast and intimate Silence—and your lips...

Faintly we saw the lanterns of three ships,
Three swaying sparks of sudden red and green...
We spoke no word; we heard unseen
A night-bird wearily flapping.
And nothing murmured in that world of wonder—
Only the hushing waters' gentle lapping.

A distant trembling, as of ghostly thunder;
Then, poignantly and plain,
The lonely whistle of a weary train...
And once again the Silence—and your lips.

Oh let me never cease to thank you for that night;
That night that eased and fortified my heart.
When radiant peace, dearer than all delight,
Bathed every old and feverish smart,
Wiped out all memories of the uncleanly fight...
Cradled in that great beauty, and your arms,
The cries and mad alarms
Were lulled and all the bitter banners furled.
The tumult vanished, and the thought thereof...
In you I knew the sweet contentment of the world,
The balm of silence and the strength of love.

IN A STRANGE CITY

Dusk—and a hunger for your face
That grows, with brooding twilight, deeper,
While in this hushed and cheerless place,
The world lies, like a careless sleeper.
Oh for a brave, red wave of sound
To send Life flowing somehow through me;
Oh for the blatant, human round
To end these hours lone and gloomy.

At last—the friendly summer night,
And children's voices calling after.
Long avenues sing out with light;
Murmurs arise and bursts of laughter.
I hear the lisp of happy feet—
Life goes by like a rushing river—
A boy comes whistling up the street...
And I am lonelier than ever.

FOLK-SONG

Back she came through the trembling dusk;
And her mother spoke and said:
"What is it makes you late to-day,
And why do you smile and sing as gay
As though you just were wed?"
"Oh mother, my hen that never had chicks
Has hatched out six!"

Back she came through the flaming dusk;
And her mother spoke and said:
"What gives your eyes that dancing light,
What makes your lips so strangely bright,
And why are your cheeks so red?"
"Oh mother, the berries I ate in the lane
Have left a stain."

Back she came through the faltering dusk;
And her mother spoke and said:
"You are weeping; your footstep is heavy with care—
What makes you totter and cling to the stair,
And why do you hang your head?"
"Oh mother—oh mother—you never can know—
I loved him so!"

IN THE STREETS

Boy, my boy, it is lonely in the city,
Days that have no pity and the nights without a tear
Follow all too slowly and I can no more dissemble;
I am frightened and I tremble—and I would that you were here.
Oh boy—God keep you.

Boy, my boy, I had sworn to weep no longer.
Time I thought was stronger than the evenings long gone by;
The ardent looks, the eager hands, the whispers hot and hurried—
But they all come back unburied and not one of them will die.
Oh boy—God save you.

Boy, my boy, you were bold with youth and power;
Your love was like a flower that you wore upon your sleeve.
And wherever you may go there'll be a girl with eyes that glisten;
A girl to watch and listen, and a girl for you to leave.
Oh boy—God help her!

ENVY

The willow and the river
Ripple with silver speech,

And one refrain forever
They murmur each to each:

"Brook with the silver gravel,
Would that your lot were mine;
To wander free, to travel
Where greener valleys shine—
Strange ventures, fresh revealings,
And, at the end—the sea!
Brook, with your turns and wheelings,
How rich your life must be."

"Tree with the golden rustling,
Would that I were so blessed,
To cease this stumbling, jostling,
This feverish unrest.
I join the ocean's riot;
You stand song-filled—and free!
Tree, with your peace and quiet,
How rich your life must be."

The willow and the river
Ripple with silver speech,
And one refrain forever
They murmur each to each.

A BIRTHDAY

Again I come
With my handful of Song—
With my trumpery gift tricked out and made showy with rhyme.
It is Spring, and the time
When your thoughts are long;
When the blossoming world in its confident prime
Whispers and wakens imperative dreams;
When you color and start
With the airiest schemes
And the laughter of children is stirring your heart...

With all of these voices that rise to restore you
To gladness again,
With your heart full of things that sing and adore you,
I come with my strain—
I come with my tinkling that patters like rain
On a rickety pane;
With a jingle of words and old tunes which have long
Done duty in song;
Spreading my verse, like a showman, before you...
And you turn to the world, as you turn to the bosom that bore you.

In all this singing at your heart,
In all this ringing through the day,
In the bravado of the May
I have no part....
For I am not one with the conquering year
That wakes without fear
The lyrical souls of the feathery throng,
That flames in the heavens when evenings are long;
That surges with power and urges with cheer
The boldness of love, the laugh of the strong,
And the confident song...

I am no longer the masterful lover
Storming my way to the shrine of your heart;
Reckless with youth and the zest to discover
All that the world sets apart.
I am no longer
Wiser and stronger;
No longer I shout in the face of the world;
No longer my challenge is sounded and hurled
With such fury that even the heavens must hear it.
No longer I mount on a passionate flood—
Something has changed my arrogant spirit,
Something has left my braggart blood.
Something has left me—something has entered in—
Something I knew not, something beyond my desire.
Deeper and gentler I hold you; all that has been
Seems like a spark that is lost in a forest of fire.
Minor my song is, for still the old memories burn—
Only in you and your thought do I find my release...
I have done with the blustering airs, and I turn
From the clamorous strife to the greater heroics of peace.

Take me again
Out of the cries and alarms
All of the tumult is vain...
Here in your arms.

Hold me again—
Oft have we wandered apart;
Now it is all made plain...
Here in your heart.

Heal me again—
Cleanse me with tears that remove
Pain and the ruins of pain...
Here in your love.

Minor my song was—abashed I must lower my voice;

Something has touched me with nobler and holier fire;
Something that thrills, as when trumpets and children rejoice;
Something I knew not, something beyond my desire...
Minor no longer—the sighing and droning depart;
In a chorus of triumph the jubilant spirits increase—
Shelter and spur me forever in the merciful strength of your heart,
You who have soothed me with passion and roused me with passionate
peace.

LEAVING THE HARBOR

At last the great, red sun sank low,
An evil, blood-shot eye,
And cooling airs sprang up to blow
The sea that challenged, glow for glow,
The angry face of the sky.

Still burned the streets we had left behind,
Where, tortured and broken down,
The millions scarcely hoped to find
A moment's escape from the maddening grind
In the terrible furnace of town.

And, blotting out cities, the twilight fell
With a single star at seven...
The sea grew wider beneath the spell
And the moon, like a broken silver shell,
Lay on the shore of heaven.

THE SHELL TO THE PEARL

Grow not so fast, glow not so warm;
Thy hidden fires burn too wild—
Too perfect is thy rounded form;
Cling close, my child.

Be yet my babe, rest quiet when
The great sea-urges beat and call;
Too soon wilt thou be ripe for men,
The world and all.

Thy shining skin, thy silken sheath,
These will undo thee all too soon;
And men will fight for thee beneath
Some paler moon...

Aye, thou my own, my undefiled,
Shalt make the lewd world dream and start,
When they have seized and torn thee, child,
Out of my heart.

With velvets shall thy bed be laid;
A royal captive thou shalt be—
And oh, what prices will be paid
To ransom thee.

Thy path shall be a track of gold,
Of lust, of death and countless crimes;
Bought by a sensual world—and sold
A thousand times...

And each shall lose thee at the last,
Hating, yet still desiring thee...
While I lie, where I have been cast,
Back in the sea.

So wait—and, lest the world transform
Thy soul and make thee wanton-wild,
Grow not so fast, glow not so warm,
Cling close, my child.

THE YOUNG MYSTIC

We sat together close and warm,
My little tired boy and I—
Watching across the evening sky
The coming of the storm.

No rumblings rose, no thunders crashed,
The west-wind scarcely sang aloud;
But from a huge and solid cloud
The summer lightnings flashed.

And then he whispered "Father, watch;
I think God's going to light His moon—"
"And when, my boy" ... "Oh, very soon—
I saw Him strike a match!"

HEALED

The winds like a pack of hounds
Snap at my dragging heels
With sudden leapings and playful bounds
They urge me out to the greener grounds
Where the butterfly sinks and the swallow reels
Giddy with Spring, with its smells and sounds—
And I go...

For of late I have fretted and sulked, and clung to my books and the house;
Lethargic with winter fancies and dulled with a torpid mood—
But now I am called by the grasses; the rumor of blossoming boughs;
The hints of a thousand singers and the ancient thrill of the wood.

For the streets run over with sunlight and spill
A glory on bricks and the dustiest sill;
And Life, like a great drum, pulses and pounds—
I follow the world and I follow my will,
And I go to see what the park reveals
When the winds, like a pack of buoyant hounds,
Snap at my dragging heels...

Once with the green again
How I am changed—
Lo, I have seen again
Friends long estranged.
Once more the lyrical
Rose-bush and river;
Once more the miracle,
Greater than ever!

Where is there dulness now—
Rich with new urges
Life in its fullness now
Surges and purges
All that is brash in me—
Sunlight and Song
These things will fashion me
Splendid and strong.

Splendid and strong I shall grow once again;
Joyful and clean as the mind of a child,
As tears after pain,
Or hearts reconciled,
As woods washed with rain,
As love in the wild,
Or that bird to whom all things but singing is vain.

"Bird, there were songs in your heart just as rapturous
As these that you bring—
Why when we longed for your magic to capture us
Did you not sing?
Now with the world making music we heed you not.
Coward, for all your fine challenge, we need you not—
We too are brave with the Spring!"

So I sang—but a something was missing; the song and the sunlight were stale,
Though a squirrel had sat on my shoulder and sparrows had fed from my hand;
Though I heard the white laughter of ripples and the breezes' faint answering hail,
And somewhere a bird's voice I knew not—yet hearing could half under-

stand...

And lo, at my doorstep I saw it; it shouted to me as I came—
It laughed in its simple revealment, a miracle common and wild;
Plainly I heard and beheld it, bright as a forest of flame—
And its face was the face of a mother, and its voice was the voice of a child.

THE STIRRUP-CUP

Your eyes—and a thousand stars
Leap from the night to aid me;
I scale the impossible bars,
I laugh at a world that dismayed me.

Your voice—and the thundering skies
Tremble and cease to appall me—
Coward no longer, I rise
Spurred for what battles may call me.

Your arms—and my purpose grows strong;
Your lips—and high passions complete me...
For your love, it is armor and Song—
And where is the thing to defeat me!

SPRING ON BROADWAY

Make way for Spring—
Spring that's a stranger in the city,
Spring that's a truant in the town.
Make way for Spring, for she has no pity
And she will tear your barriers down—
Make way for Spring!

See from her hidden valleys,
With mirth that never palls,
She comes with songs and sallies,
With bells and magic calls,
And dances down your alleys,
And whispers through your walls.

You who never once have missed her
In your town of pomp and pride
Now in vain you will resist her—
You will feel her at your side;
Even in the smallest street,
Even in the densest throng,
She will follow at your feet,
She will walk with you along.
She will stop you as you start
Here and there, and growing bolder,

She will touch you on the shoulder,
She will clutch you at the heart...

Merchant, you who drink your mead
From a golden cup,
Shut your ears, and do not heed;
Look not up.
Beware—for she is light as air,
And her charm will work confusion;
Spring is but an old delusion
And a snare....
Merchant, you who drink your mead
While the thirsty die,
Shut your eyes, and do not heed—
Pass her by.

Maiden with the nun-like eyes
Do not pause to greet her;
Spring is far too wild and wise—
Do not meet her.
Do not listen while she tells
Her persuasive lures and spells;
Do not learn her secrets, lest
She should plant them in your breast;
Whisper things to shame and shock you,
Make your heart beat fast—and mock you;
Send you dreams that rob your rest...
Maiden with the nun-like eyes
Spring is far too wild and wise.

And you, my friend, with hasty stride
Think you to escape her;
Ah, like fire touching paper,
She will burn into your side.
She will rouse you once again;
She will sway you, till you follow
Like the smallest singing swallow
In her train.

Put irons on your feet, my friend,
And chain your soul with golden weights,
Lest she should move you in the end
And lead you past the city gates;
And make you frolic with the wind;
And play a thousand godlike parts;
And sing—until within you starts
A pity for the senseless blind,
The deaf, the dumb and all their kind
Whose eager, aimless footsteps wind

Forever to the frantic marts,
Through every mad and breathless street..,
My friend, put irons on your feet.

So—and that is right, my friend;
Do not yield.
Send her on her way, and end
All her follies; let her spend
Her reckless days and nights concealed
In wood and field......
The paths beyond the town are clear;
These skies are wan—
Bid her begone.
What is she doing here?

What is she doing here—and why?
The city is no place for Spring.
What can she have; what can she bring
That you would care to buy.
Her songs? Alas, you do not sing.
Her smiles? You have no time to try.
Her wings? You do not care to fly—
Spring has not fashioned anything
To tempt your jaded eye.

The city is no place for her—
It is too violent and shrill;
Too full of graver things—but still
Beneath the throbbing surge and stir,
Her spirit lives and moves, until
Even the dullest feel the spur
Of an awakened will.

Make way then—Life, rejoicing,
Calls, with a lyric rout,
Till in this mighty voicing
The very stones sing out;
Till nowhere is a single
Sleeping or silent thing,
And worlds that meet and mingle
Fairly tingle with the Spring.

Make way for Her—
For the fervor of Life,
For the passions that stir,
For the courage of Strife;
For the struggles that bring
A more vivid day—
Make way for Spring;

Make way!

IN A CAB

Rain—and the lights of the city,
Blurred by the mist on the pane.
A thing without passion or pity—
This is the rain.

It beats on the roof with derision,
It howls at the doors of the cab—
Phantoms go by in a vision,
Distorted and drab.

Torpor and dreariness greet me;
All of the things I abhor
Rise to confront and defeat me,
As I ride to your door...

At last you have come; you have banished
The gloom of each rain-haunted street—
The tawdry surroundings have vanished;
The evening is sweet.

Now the whole city is dreamlike;
The rain plays the lightest of tunes;
The lamps through the mist make it seem like
A city of moons.

No longer my fancies run riot;
I hold the most magic of charms—
You smile at me, warm and unquiet,
Here in my arms.

I do not wonder or witness
Whether it rains or is fair;
I only can think of your sweetness,
And the scent of your hair.

I am deaf to the clatter and drumming,
And life is a thing to ignore...
Alas, my beloved, we are coming
Once more to your door!...

You have gone; it is listless and lonely;
The evening is empty again;
The world is a blank—there is only
The desolate rain.

SUMMER NIGHT—BROADWAY

Night is the city's disease.
The streets and the people one sees
Glow with a light that is strangely inhuman;
A fever that never grows cold.
Heaven completes the disgrace;
For now, with her star-pitted face,
Night has the leer of a dissolute woman,
Cynical, moon-scarred and old.

And I think of the country roads;
Of the quiet, sleeping abodes,
Where every tree is a silent brother
And the hearth is a thing to cling to.
And I sicken and long for it now—
To feel clean winds on my brow,
Where Night bends low, like an all-wise mother
Looking for children to sing to.

HAUNTED

Between the moss and stone
The lonely lilies rise;
Wasted and overgrown
The tangled garden lies.
Weeds climb about the stoop
And clutch the crumbling walls;
The drowsy grasses droop—
The night wind falls.

The place is like a wood;
No sign is there to tell
Where rose and iris stood
That once she loved so well.
Where phlox and asters grew,
A leafless thornbush stands,
And shrubs that never knew
Her tender hands...

Over the broken fence
The moonbeams trail their shrouds;
Their tattered cerements
Cling to the gauzy clouds,
In ribbons frayed and thin—
And startled by the light,
Silence shrinks deeper in
The depths of night.

Useless lie spades and rakes;

Rust's on the garden-tools.
Yet, where the moonlight makes
Nebulous silver pools,
A ghostly shape is cast—
Something unseen has stirred.
Was it a breeze that passed?
Was it a bird?

Dead roses lift their heads
Out of a grassy tomb;
From ruined pansy-beds
A thousand pansies bloom.
The gate is opened wide—
The garden that has been,
Now blossoms like a bride...
Who entered in?

ISADORA DUNCAN DANCING
"IPHIGENIA IN AULIS"

1

Fling the stones and let them all
Lie;
Take a breath, and toss the ball
High—
And before it strikes the floor
Of the hoar and aged shore,
Sweep them up, though there should be
Even more than two or three.

Add a pebble, then once more
Fling the stones and let them all
Lie;
Take a breath, and toss the ball
High....

2

Rises now the sound of ancient chants
And the circling figure moves more slowly.
Thus the stately gods themselves must dance
While the world grows rapturous and holy.
Thus the gods might weave a great Romance
Singing to the sighs of flute and psalter;
Till the last of all the many chants,
And the priestess sinks before the altar.

3

Cease, oh cease the murmured singing;
Hush the numbers brave or blithe,
For she enters gravely swinging,
Lowering and lithe—
Dark and vengeful as the ringing
Scythe meets scythe.

While the flame is fiercely sweeping
All her virgin airs depart;
She is, without smiles and weeping
Or a maiden's art,
Stern and savage as the leaping
Heart meets heart!

4

Now the tune grows frantic,
Now the torches flare—
Wild and corybantic
Echoes fill the air.
With a sudden sally
All the voices shout;
And the bacchic rally
Turns into a rout.

Here is life that surges
Through each burning vein;
Here is joy that purges
Every creeping pain.
Even sober Sadness
Casts aside her pall,
Till with buoyant madness
She must swoon and fall...

CHOPIN

Faint preludings on a flute
And she swims before us;
Shadows follow in pursuit,
Like a phantom chorus.
Sense and sound are intertwined
Through her necromancy,
Till our dreaming souls are blind
To all things but fancy.

Haunted woods and perfumed nights,
Swift and soft desires,
Roses, violet-colored lights,

And the sound of lyres,
Vague chromatics on a flute—
All are subtly blended,
Till the instrument grows mute
And the dance is ended.

SONGS AND THE POET

(For Sara Teasdale)

Sing of the rose or of the mire; sing strife
Or rising moons; the silence or the throng...
Poet, it matters not, if Life
Is in the song.

If Life rekindles it, and if the rhymes
Bear Beauty as their eloquent refrain,
Though it were sung a thousand times,
Sing it again!

Thrill us with song—let others preach or rage;
Make us so thirst for Beauty that we cease
These struggles, and this strident age
Grows sweet with peace.

THE HERETIC

I. BLASPHEMY

I do not envy God—
There is no thing in all the skies or under
To startle and awaken Him to wonder;
No marvel can appear
To stir His placid soul with terrible thunder—
He was not born with awe nor blessed with fear.

I do not envy God—
He is not burned with Spring and April madness;
The rush of Life—its rash, impetuous gladness
He cannot hope to know.
He cannot feel the fever and the sadness
The leaping fire, the insupportable glow.

I do not envy God—
Forever He must watch the planets crawling
To flaming goals where sun and star are falling;
He cannot wander free.
For He must face, through centuries appalling,
A vast and infinite monotony.

I do not envy God—
He cannot die, He dare not even slumber.

Though He be God and free from care and cumber,
I would not share His place;
For He must live when years have lost their number
And Time sinks crumbling into shattered Space.

I do not envy God—
Nay more, I pity Him His lonely heaven;
I pity Him each lonely morn and even,
His splendid lonely throne:
For He must sit and wait till all is riven
Alone—through all eternity—alone.

II. IRONY

Why are the things that have no death
The ones with neither sight nor breath.
Eternity is thrust upon
A bit of earth, a senseless stone.
A grain of dust, a casual clod
Receives the greatest gift of God.
A pebble in the roadway lies—
It never dies.

The grass our fathers cut away
Is growing on their graves to-day;
The tiniest brooks that scarcely flow
Eternally will come and go.
There is no kind of death to kill
The sands that lie so meek and still...
But Man is great and strong and wise—
And so he dies.

III. MOCKERY

God, I return to you on April days
When along country-roads you walk with me;
And my faith blossoms like the earliest tree
That shames the bleak world with its yellow sprays.
My faith revives when, through a rosy haze,
The clover-sprinkled hills smile quietly;
Young winds uplift a bird's clean ecstacy...
For this, oh God, my joyousness and praise.

But now—the crowded streets and choking airs,
The huddled thousands bruised and tossed about—
These, or the over-brilliant thoroughfares,
The too-loud laughter and the empty shout;
The mirth-mad city, tragic with its cares...
For this, oh God, my silence—and my doubt.

IV. HUMILITY

Oh God, if I have ever been
So filled with ignorance and sin
That I have dared to use Thy name
In blasphemy, in jest, in shame;
If ever I have dared to flout
Thy works, and mock Thy deeds with doubt,
Thou must forgive me as Thou art divine
For, God, the fault was Thine as well as mine.

Oh, I have used Thee, time on time,
To fill a phrase, to round a rhyme;
But was this wrong? Nay, in Thy heart
Thou knowest the noble theme Thou art...
Was it my fault that as I sung
The daring speech was on my tongue?
Nay; if my singing, God, gave Thee offense,
Thou wouldst have robbed me of the lyric sense.

But dignity hath made Thee dumb,
And so Thou biddest me to come
And be a sonant part of Thee;
To sing Thy praise in blasphemy,
To be the life within the clod
That points the paradox of God.
To chant, beneath a loud and lyric grief,
A faith that flaunts its very disbelief.

FIFTH AVENUE—SPRING AFTERNOON

The world's running over with color,
With whispers, strange fervors and April—
There's a smell in the air as if meadows
Were under our feet.

Spring smiles at the commonest waysides;
But she pours out her heart to the city,
As one woman might to another
Who meet after years...

Restless with color and perfume,
The streets are a riot of blossoms.
What garden could boast of such flowers—
Not Eden itself.

Primroses, pinks and gardenias,
Shame the gray town and its squalor—
Windows are flaming with jonquils;
Fires of gold!

Out of a florist's some pansies
Peer at the crowd, like the faces
Of solemnly mischievous children
Going to bed...

And women—Spring's favorite children—
Frail and phantastically fashioned,
Pass like a race of immortals,
Too radiant for earth.

The pale and the drab are transfigured,
They sing themselves into the sunshine—
Every girl is a lyric,
An urge and a lure.

And, like a challenge of trumpets,
The Spring and its impulse goes through me—
Breezes and flowers and people
Sing in my blood...

Breezes and flowers and people—
And under it all, oh beloved,
Out of the song and the sunshine,
Rises your face!

TRIBUTE

Never will you let me
Tire of leaping passion;
Never can I grow weary
Of undesired joys.

The delicate strength of your bosom;
Your hands' incredible softness;
The fluent curve of your body;
The fierceness of your lips;

Ceaselessly do they call me—
You and your eloquent beauty
Are challenge and invitation
Too ravishing to resist.

Always the burning summons,
The sweet, imperative madness,
Rides over me, like a conqueror,
Careless and confident...

Even so goes Love,
Trampling and invincible;
With rapt and pitiless beauty,
Rough-shod over the world!

III
SONGS OF PROTEST

To
James Oppenheim

CHALLENGE

The quiet and courageous night,
The keen vibration of the stars,
Call me, from morbid peace, to fight
The world's forlorn and desperate wars.

The air throbs like a rolling drum —
The brave hills and the singing sea,
Unrest and people's faces come
Like battle-trumpets, rousing me.

And while Life's lusty banner flies,
I shall assail, with raging mirth,
The scornful and untroubled skies,
The cold complacency of earth.

CALIBAN IN THE COAL MINES

God, we don't like to complain
We know that the mine is no lark—
But—there's the pools from the rain;
But—there's the cold and the dark.

God, You don't know what it is—
You, in Your well-lighted sky,
Watching the meteors whizz;
Warm, with the sun always by.

God, if You had but the moon
Stuck in Your cap for a lamp,
Even You'd tire of it soon,
Down in the dark and the damp.

Nothing but blackness above,
And nothing that moves but the cars—
God, if You wish for our love,
Fling us a handful of stars!

ANY CITY

Into the staring street
She goes on her nightly round,
With weary and tireless feet

Over the wretched ground.

A thing that man never spurns,
A thing that all men despise;
Into her soul there burns
The street with its pitiless eyes.

She needs no charm or wile,
She carries no beauty or power,
But a tawdry and casual smile
For a tawdry and casual hour.

The street with its pitiless eyes
Follows wherever she lurks,
But she is hardened and wise—
She rattles her bracelets and smirks...

She goes with her sordid array,
Luring, without a lure;
She is man's hunger and prey—
His lust and its hideous cure.

All that she knows are the lies,
The evil, the squalor, the scars;
The street with its pitiless eyes,
The night with its pitiless stars.

LANDSCAPES

(For Clement R. Wood)

The rain was over, and the brilliant air
Made every little blade of grass appear
Vivid and startling—everything was there
With sharpened outlines, eloquently clear,
As though one saw it in a crystal sphere.
The rusty sumac with its struggling spires;
The golden-rod with all its million fires;
(A million torches swinging in the wind)
A single poplar, marvellously thinned,
Half like a naked boy, half like a sword;
Clouds, like the haughty banners of the Lord;
A group of pansies with their shrewish faces,
Little old ladies cackling over laces;
The quaint, unhurried road that curved so well;
The prim petunias with their rich, rank smell;
The lettuce-birds, the creepers in the field—
How bountifully were they all revealed!
How arrogantly each one seemed to thrive—
So frank and strong, so radiantly alive!

And over all the morning-minded earth
There seemed to spread a sharp and kindling mirth,
Piercing the stubborn stones until I saw
The toad face heaven without shame or awe,
The ant confront the stars, and every weed
Grow proud as though it bore a royal seed;
While all the things that die and decompose
Sent forth their bloom as richly as the rose...
Oh, what a liberal power that made them thrive
And keep the very dirt that died, alive.

And now I saw the slender willow-tree
No longer calm or drooping listlessly,
Letting its languid branches sway and fall
As though it danced in some sad ritual;
But rather like a young, athletic girl,
Fearless and gay, her hair all out of curl,
And flying in the wind—her head thrown back,
Her arms flung up, her garments flowing slack,
And all her rushing spirits running over...
What made a sober tree seem such a rover—
Or made the staid and stalwart apple-trees,
That stood for years knee-deep in velvet peace,
Turn all their fruit to little worlds of flame,
And burn the trembling orchard there below.
What lit the heart of every golden-glow—
Oh, why was nothing weary, dull or tame?...
Beauty it was, and keen, compassionate mirth
That drives the vast and energetic earth.

And, with abrupt and visionary eyes,
I saw the huddled tenements arise.
Here where the merry clover danced and shone
Sprang agonies of iron and of stone;
There, where green Silence laughed or stood enthralled,
Cheap music blared and evil alleys sprawled.
The roaring avenues, the shrieking mills;
Brothels and prisons on those kindly hills—
The menace of these things swept over me;
A threatening, unconquerable sea...

A stirring landscape and a generous earth!
Freshening courage and benevolent mirth—
And then the city, like a hideous sore...
Good God, and what is all this beauty for?

TWO FUNERALS

I.

Upon a field of shrieking red
A mighty general stormed and fell.
They raised him from the common dead
And all the people mourned him well.
"Swiftly," they cried, "let honors come,
And Glory with her deathless bays;
For him let every muffled drum
And grieving bugle thrill with praise.
Has he not made the whole world fear
The very lifting of his sword—
Has he not slain his thousands here
To glorify the Law and Lord!
Then make his bed of sacred sod;
To greater deeds no man can win"...
And each amused and ancient god
Began to grin.

II.

Facing a cold and sneering sky,
Cold as the sneering hearts of men,
A man began to prophesy,
To speak of love and faith again.
Boldly he spoke, and bravely dared
The savage jest, the kindlier stone;
The armies mocked at him; he fared
To battle gaily—and alone.
Alone he fought; alone, to move
A world whose wars would never cease—
And all his blows were struck for love,
And all his fighting was for peace...
They tortured him with thorns and rods,
They hanged him on a frowning hill—
And all the old and heartless gods
Are laughing still.

SUNDAY

It was Sunday—
Eleven in the morning; people were at church—
Prayers were in the making; God was near at hand—
Down the cramped and narrow streets of quiet Lawrence
Came the tramp of workers marching in their hundreds;
Marching in the morning, marching to the grave-yard,

Where, no longer fiery, underneath the grasses,
Callous and uncaring, lay their friend and sister.
In their hands they carried wreaths and drooping flowers,
Overhead their banners dipped and soared like eagles—

Aye, but eagles bleeding, stained with their own heart's-blood—
Red, but not for glory—red, with wounds and travail,
Red, the buoyant symbol of the blood of all the world...
So they bore their banners, singing toward the grave-yard,
So they marched and chanted, mingling tears and tributes,
So, with flowers, the dying went to deck the dead.

Within the churches people heard
The sound, and much concern was theirs—
God might not hear the Sacred Word—
God might not hear their prayers!

Should such things be allowed these slaves—
To vex the Sabbath peace with Song,
To come with chants, like marching waves,
That proudly swept along...

Suppose God turned to these—and heard!
Suppose He listened unawares—
God might forget the Sacred Word,
God might forget their prayers!

And so (oh, tragic irony)
The blue-clad Guardians of the Peace
Were sent to sweep them back—to see
The ribald song should cease;

To scatter those who came and vexed
God with their troubled cries and cares.
Quiet—so God might hear the text;
The sleek and unctuous prayers!

Up the rapt and singing streets of little Lawrence,
Came the stolid soldiers; and, behind the blue-coats,
Grinning and invisible, bearing unseen torches,
Rode red hordes of anger, sweeping all before them.
Lust and Evil joined them—Terror rode among them;
Fury fired its pistols; Madness stabbed and yelled...
Through the wild and bleeding streets of shuddering Lawrence,
Raged the heedless panic, hour-long and bitter.
Passion tore and trampled; men once mild and peaceful,
Fought with savage hatred in the name of Law and Order.
And, below the outcry, like the sea beneath the breakers,
Mingling with the anguish, rolled the solemn organ...

Eleven in the morning—people were at church—

Prayers were in the making—God was near at hand—
It was Sunday!

STRIKERS

In the mud and scum of things,
Underneath the whole world's blot,
Something, they tell us, always sings—
Why do we hear it not?

In the heart of things unclean,
Somewhere, in the furious fight,
The face of God is plainly seen—
What has destroyed our sight?

Yet have we heard enough to feel,
Yet have we seen enough to know
Who bound us to the awful wheel,
Whose hands have brought us low.

And we shall cry out till the wind
Roars in their ears the thing to come—
Yea, though they made us deaf and blind,
Nothing shall keep us dumb!

IN THE SUBWAY

Chaos is tamed and ordered as we ride;
The rock is rent, the darkness flung aside
And all the horrors of the deep defied.

A coil of wires, a throb, a sudden spark—
And on a screaming meteor we embark
That hurls us past the cold and breathless dark.

The centuries disclose their secret graves—
Riding in splendor through a world of waves
The ancient elements become our slaves.

Uncanny fancies whisper to and fro;
Terror and Night surround us here below,
And through the house of Death we come and go...

And here, oh wildest glimpse of all, I see
The score of men and women facing me
Reading their papers calmly, leisurely.

BATTLE-CRIES

Yes, Jim hez gone—ye didn't know?
He's fightin' at the front.
It's him as bears 'his country's hopes'.

An' me as bears the brunt.

Wen war bruk out Jim 'lowed he'd go—
He allus loved a scrap—
Ye see, the home warn't jest the place
Fer sech a lively chap.

O' course, the work seems ruther hard;
The kids is ruther small—
It ain't that I am sore at Jim,
I envy him—that's all.

He doesn't know what he's about
An' cares still less, does Jim...
With all his loose an' roarin' ways
I wisht that I was him.

It makes him glad an' drunken-like
That music an' the smoke;
An' w'en they shout, the whole thing seems
A picnic an' a joke.

Oh, yellin' puts a heart in ye,
An' stren'th into yer blows—
I wisht that I could hears those cheers
Washin' the neighbors clo'es...

It's funny how some things work out—
Life is so strange, Lord love us—
Here am I, workin' night an' day
To keep a roof above us;

An' Jim is somewhere in the south,
An' Jim ain't really bad,
A-runnin' round an' raisin' Cain,
An' stabbin' some kid's dad.

But that's w'at men are made for—eh?
W'at else is there for me
But workin' on till Jim comes home,
Sick of his bloody spree.

A VOICE FROM THE SWEAT-SHOPS

(A HYMN WITH RESPONSES)

"Praise God from Whom all blessings flow;
Praise Him all creatures here below.
Every morning mercies new
Fall as fresh as morning dew."

Yet we are choked with sin
With bestial lusts and guile;

God (so it runs) made this world clean
And Man has made it vile.

Aye, here Man lives on man,
And breaks him day by day—
But in the trampled jungle
The tiger claws his prey.

God's curse is on the thief;
The murderer fares ill—
Who gave the beasts their taste for blood
Who taught them how to kill?

"All praise to Him Who built the hills,
All praise to Him Who each stream fills;
All praise to Him Who lights each star
That sparkles in the sky afar."

All praise to Him who made
The earthquake and the flood;
All praise to Him who made the pest
That sucks away the blood.

All praise to Him whose mind
Had the desire to make
The shark, the scorpion, the gnat
And the envenomed snake.

Beauty itself He turns
To slay and to be slain—
A thousand evil poisons
His peaceful woods contain.

"Lift up your heart! Lift up your voice!
Rejoice! Again I say, rejoice!
For His mercies, they are sure
His compassion will endure!"

Rejoice because each man
Has but a man's desire
To sin the little human sins
As a child that plays with fire.

Rejoice because God's plans
Are far too deep for talk...
He lets the swallow feed on flies—
Then gives it to the hawk!

Rejoice because He made
A world in some wild mood;
A world that feeds upon itself—
'And God saw it was good...'

Yet who are we to rail—
Vainly we strive and storm—
God moves in a mysterious way
His wonders to perform!

'Blind unbelief is sure to err,'
They say, and yet again,
'God is His own interpreter'—
When will He make it plain?

SOLDIERS

Gay flags flying down the street;
Comes the drum's insistent beat
Like a fierce, gigantic pulse,
And the screaming fife exults.

Soldier, soldier, spic and span,
Aren't you the lucky man;
Splendid in your gold and blue—
How the small boy envies you!

Oh, there's glory for you here—
Girls to smile and men to cheer;
Bands behind and bands before
Thrilling with the lust of War.

Soldier, soldier, proud as though
Marching to a sanguine foe,
Bravely would you face the brink
Fired with music, and with drink...

Stalwart warrior pass, and be
Glad you are not such as we—
We, who, without flags or drums,
March to battle in the slums.

Regiments of workers—we
Are a foolish soldiery,
Combating, till we convert,
Ignorance, disease and dirt...

Soldier, soldier, look—and then
Laugh at us poor fighting-men,
Struggling on, though every street
Is the scene of our defeat.

Laugh at us, who, day by day
Come back beaten from the fray;
We, who find our work undone—
We, whose wars are never won.

Gay flags flying down the street;
Comes the drum's insistent beat
Like a fierce, gigantic pulse—
And the screaming fife exults!

PEACE

(The Fisheries dispute having been amicably compromised, the world is at peace again.   .... News Despatch.)

'At peace'? The world has never been at peace—
Its wars are never-ending; there is naught
In all its battles like these overwrought
And storming hours with their dark increase.
The cities roar; in every street one sees
Women and children, battle-wounded, caught.—
No slaves, no shattered hosts have ever fought
So bitterly, so hopeless of release...

Well, if it must be war, take up the sword,
Facing the world with grim and savage glee;
And, with the courage of a Faith restored,
Strike till the darkness falters, and we see
That liberty is no mere gaudy word,
And peace no slothful, placid mockery.

THE DYING DECADENT

And when the evening came he fell asleep,
And dreamed a dream of pallid loveliness:

He wandered in a forest dark and deep,
Where phantoms passed him with a soft caress;
Where shadows moved and ghostly spirits stood
Sphinxes of silence, wraiths of mystery;
A magic wood, a strange and scented wood
Where roses sprang from every withered tree.
A wood that woke his wonder and his fear,
A wood of whispered spells and shameful lore,
Beyond whose furthest rim he seemed to hear
A lonely sea upon a lonelier shore.
Visions swept by him with a chanted spell,
Crouched at his feet and murmured at his side—
And like a dim refrain there rose and fell
The restless minor of an ebbing tide...
Then, amidst broken sighs and wafts of song,
Borne on the breezes blowing from the west,
He saw one figure dancing in the throng
More wan and wonderful than all the rest.

The singing grew and nearer still she came,
A being made of rose and fire and mist;
Her deep eyes burning like the purple flame
Hid in the heart of every amethyst.
And, with the crooning of the distant sea,
She sang to charm his soul and still his fear:
"Oh, come, my love that wanders wearily;
Oh, come, for you have called, and I am here...
Oh, I have waited long to bring you there,
Beyond the border of the things that are,
Where all is terrible and strange and fair,
As were your dreams that reached my favorite star...
For you shall live and set the suns to rhyme;
You shall escape a mortal's petty fate;
You shall behold the birth and death of Time...
Oh come, my love, for you these wonders wait.

"Moonlight and music and the sound of waves,
Sea-spells incanted by a mermaid-muse,
And women's voices breathing slumb'rous staves,
These shall you have whenever you may choose.
And you shall know the maidens of the moon,
Lying on lilies shall you see them dance;
And you shall fling red roses to the tune,
Great roses while the magic scene enchants.
Wantons and queens shall take your heart to play
And lose it in a mesh of tangled hair;
And you shall always give your heart away,
And find a new one every hour there.
Here are the notes of every nightingale
Like rare pearls dropping in a golden pan;
And you shall hear white music in each dale,
Sweet silver sounds that are not heard by man.
And I shall show you all the world's delight,
The unknown passion of each flaming star;
Your eyes shall be endowed with keener sight
Beyond the border of the things that are.
Oh come, they wait you on the further strand—
Your drab and mournful mood they will exchange
For joy's resplendent purple in the land
Where all is rhythmical and fair and strange...
Oh come and learn the songs unborn, unsung,
And I shall give you all your longing craves,
That you may live in ecstasy among
Moonlight and music and the sound of waves."

Entranced he stood—so exquisite the art

That charmed him he could scarcely whisper low:
"And who are you that comes to stir my heart
With fragments of the songs I used to know — —
You speak of wild and yet familiar things,
Exotic passions and uncanny bliss;
A thousand dreams your voice recalls and brings;
And who are you that shows me all of this?"
"I am the soul and spirit of your songs;
I am your ballad's grief, your lyric's fire.
I am the light for which your yearning longs;
Your curious rapture and your sick desire.
I am the burden that your lays beseech;
The one refrain that flows through all your themes.
I am the eerie glamor of your speech,
I am the mystic radiance of your dreams.
Come then with me, where all men's dreams are born,
Where winds shall lift your perfumed thoughts aloft;
Where there is never night or noon or morn,
Only a twilight, sensuous and soft.
And you shall know the wonder of each year,
The fiery secrets of a myriad Springs...
Lying on lilies shall you see them here;
And you shall live and touch immortal things."

She paused and sighed. Slowly he shook his head
As one who sees a guarded flame go out;
"Never to die? Nay that alone," he said,
"Were worse than all this wandering in doubt.
Nor would I go if Death himself should come
To crown Life's blessing with a greater gift;
In such a perfect world I would be dumb—
What could I long for when my fancies drift?...
And more than this, I do not choose to go;
For I am sick of strange and subtle sounds,
Of fevered phrases, tinted words that glow,
And all the twisting art that but astounds.
I do not long for tortured harmonies;
No more my languid soul is racked and tossed
With yearning for strange shores and stranger seas—
I seek the visions I have long since lost.
I seek the ways of simple love and hate,
Once more I long to join the virile race;
For I was blind till now, and now too late
I see the wonder of the commonplace.

"I long to hear men's voices, coarse and wild,
That never knew a poet's wan desire;

I long to hear them, as a little child
Listens to elders grouped about the fire...
To hear them as they mingle grave and gay—
The prudent planning for the week, and then
Amid the tritest gossip of the day,
Quaint, petty talk of merchandise and men.
I crave the usual and homely themes;
The everyday of which no mermaid sings....
These are the fairest fragments of my dreams;
These are the conquering and deathless things."

He ceased; a sudden radiance round him shone,
And all things melted like a phantom wrack.
And as he swept his hands and stood alone
He heard hoarse thunders and the dusk grew black.
Vast tremors shook the world from side to side—
The earth and sky became a monstrous blot...

And then it seems he woke, and waking, died;
Calling on things that he had long forgot.

FUNERAL HYMN

When Life's gay courage fails at last,
And I grow worse than old—
Though Death puts out my fiery heart,
I never shall grow cold.

For warm is earth's green covering,
And warmly I shall lie,
Wrapped in the winding-sheets of air
And the great, blue folds of sky!

PROTESTS

(After a Painting by Hugo Ballin)

Something impelled her from the hearth;
Whispers and winds drew her along;
But still, unconscious of the earth,
She read her book of golden Song.

Old legends stirred her as she read
Of life victoriously unfurled,
Of glories gone but never dead,
And Beauty that redeemed the world.

"Oh Songs," she sighed, "your world was fair;
My own holds no such lovely things;
No glow, no magic anywhere—"
And then, a start—a flash of wings...

And, with the rush of surging seas,
Over her swept the world's replies:
The lyric hills, the buoyant breeze
And all the sudden singing skies!

Lector House believes that a society develops through a two-fold approach of continuous learning and adaptation, which is derived from the study of classic literary works spread across the historic timeline of literature records. Therefore, we aim at reviving, repairing and redeveloping all those inaccessible or damaged but historically as well as culturally important literature across subjects so that the future generations may have an opportunity to study and learn from past works to embark upon a journey of creating a better future.

This book is a result of an effort made by Lector House towards making a contribution to the preservation and repair of original ancient works which might hold historical significance to the approach of continuous learning across subjects.

HAPPY READING & LEARNING!

LECTOR HOUSE LLP
E-MAIL: lectorpublishing@gmail.com

9 789354 208645